NAVIGATE YOUR WAY TO A SECURE RETIREMENT

A Retiree's Guide to Removing Roadblocks
and Hazards While Gaining Confidence
and Peace of Mind

T0145730

NAVIGATE
YOUR WAY TO A
SECURE RETIREMENT

A Retiree's Guide to Removing Roadblocks and Hazards While Gaining Confidence and Peace of Mind

ISAAC WRIGHT

Jean Reynolds, contributor

Published by Advantage, Charleston, South Carolina.
Member of Advantage Media Group.

ADVANTAGE is a registered trademark and the Advantage colophon is a trademark of Advantage Media Group, Inc.

Printed in the United States of America.

ISBN: 978-159932-283-4
LCCN: 2011910654

This publication is designed to provide accurate and authoritative information in regard to the subject matter covered. It is sold with the understanding that the publisher is not engaged in rendering legal, accounting, or other professional services. If legal advice or other expert assistance is required, the services of a competent professional person should be sought.

Advantage Media Group is proud to be a part of the Tree Neutral® program. Tree Neutral offsets the number of trees consumed in the production and printing of this book by taking proactive steps such as planting trees in direct proportion to the number of trees used to print books. To learn more about Tree Neutral, please visit www.treeneutral.com. To learn more about Advantage's commitment to being a responsible steward of the environment, please visit www.advantagefamily.com/green

Advantage Media Group is a leading publisher of business, motivation, and self-help authors. Do you have a manuscript or book idea that you would like to have considered for publication? Please visit www.amgbook.com or call 1.866.775.1696

ABOUT THE AUTHOR

 **ISAAC WRIGHT** is a financial planner specializing in retirement planning and asset preservation for families and retirees. He is the President and CEO of Financial Dynamics and the Estate and Elder Planning Center of Virginia, located in the Richmond area.

Isaac has been assisting families and retirees reach their financial, retirement and estate planning goals for over a decade, building a reputation among his clients and colleagues as a personally engaged problem solver who provides exceptional customer service.

Working with other advisors, attorneys and caregivers, Isaac's approach is inclusive, transparent and education-based. Widely recognized in Virginia and beyond as a specialist in retirement planning, Isaac frequently appears on television, radio, webcasts and in public seminars focusing on financial and legal retirement planning, the economics of long-term healthcare and asset preservation. His blog, *Wright Advice for Your Money,* can be found at www.wrightmoneyadvice.com.

Isaac has been a member and contributor of several mentoring and private coaching groups, including Ed Slott's

Elite IRA group and the Longevity Planning Institute. He is also a member of the National Ethics Bureau.

A lifelong resident of the Richmond area, Isaac is a graduate of Virginia Commonwealth University.

Investment Advisory Services offered through Global Financial Private Capital, LLC, an SEC Registered Investment Advisor.

 **CONTRIBUTOR JEAN REYNOLDS,** attorney at law, is a partner at Whitehead and Chiocca PLC, in Richmond, Virginia.

Jean specializes in estate planning, asset protection, wills and trusts, special needs planning, estate administration and litigation. She earned her Juris Doctor from the Appalachian School of Law and is a member of the Virginia State Bar.

Jean is a former president of the Richmond chapter of the Society of Financial Services Professionals and a member of the Richmond area Estate Planning Council.

CONTENTS

that the capacity to enjoy your retirement years, regardless of health or financial circumstances, is far too precious to leave to chance.

CHAPTER 1

A FALSE SENSE OF SECURITY

Medicare can be a godsend when it comes to medical necessities and acute care, but remember: **Medicare is health insurance, not long-term care insurance** *—and you might be surprised what it covers and what it doesn't. Know the rules of the road and plan accordingly.*

How to pay for the rising costs of healthcare premiums and medical costs can arguably be the financial focal point for anybody today, regardless of age. The concern seems particularly skewed to an aging population that continues to live longer than ever before.

Medicare has come as a godsend to individuals and families who could not otherwise afford even basic healthcare during their retirement years.

That said, it is critical to understand what exactly Medicare covers. We all will face medical issues as we age, from minor aches and pains to problems requiring full-time, skilled nursing care. This is illustrated with a great visual on pages 16 and 17, which brings to light different stages in someone's health in

All of this seems straightforward enough, so why are so many people blind-sided when Medicare stops paying the bills? In most cases, the trouble starts when the need arises for non-rehabilitative or custodial care services.

relation to what or who will pay for medical care. With this in mind, let's review what Medicare does and why it is so important to both your financial and physical well-being.

Medicare is health insurance for people age 65 or older, under age 65 with certain disabilities, and any age with permanent kidney failure (called "end-stage renal disease")[1]. The program was established in 1965 to help pay the cost of hospitalization, doctors and medical expenses for elderly and disabled persons. It still operates under the same premise today.

Medicare is made up of two major parts, A and B, and two

So what happens when you have to leave the hospital? Depending on where you go and what type of care you are receiving, the maximum amount of time that Medicare will continue to pay for rehab or recovery services is 100 days.

---

secondary parts, C and D. Part A (hospital insurance) helps pay for inpatient hospital care, skilled nursing care, hospice care and other services. Part B (medical insurance) helps pay for doctors' fees, outpatient hospital visits, and other medical services and supplies. Part C (Medicare Advantage) plans allow

---

[1]Center of Medicare and Medicaid Services, publication #11306

Elder C

| Healthy Vigorous Senior | Medications and Chronic Health Problems | Hospitalization | Declin Senior Mobil Issue |

Medicare "Cares"
(Acute Care) &
Private Insurance
& Private Pay Deductible

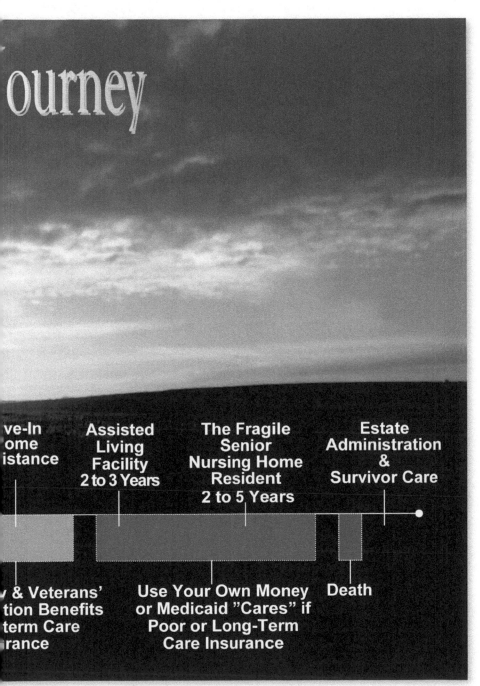

ourney

ve-In
ome
istance

**Assisted
Living
Facility**
2 to 3 Years

**The Fragile
Senior
Nursing Home
Resident**
2 to 5 Years

**Estate
Administration
&
Survivor Care**

& Veterans'
tion Benefits
term Care
rance

**Use Your Own Money
or Medicaid "Cares" if
Poor or Long-Term
Care Insurance**

Death

Image courtesy of Rick Law

17

you to choose to receive all of your healthcare services through a provider organization, such as a PPO or an HMO.

Medicare Part D (prescription drug coverage) offers enrollment in prescription plans that can lower the cost of medications. With people living longer, almost everyone will take some form of blood pressure pill, cholesterol pill, or use other medications to help control common conditions as we age. Even though Medicare does not cover all prescription medication expenses, this program brings savings to many who take multiple medications as they grow older.

I see numerous seniors and retirees who have had great experiences with Medicare covering all or nearly all costs associated with doctors' fees, hospital visits and even complex procedures such as knee replacements or bypass surgery. A medically necessary, acute care issue is when Medicare shines bright for people in this phase of life.

Even active seniors with mobility issues can use Medicare for assistance. Remember the television commercial for the scooter store? What was their pitch—something like, "Call us, and if Medicare will not cover the costs of your scooter, how much will you have to pay? That's right, nothing!" They had to feel real confident about Medicare covering the scooter, or else they would have gone broke giving away free ones!

All of this seems straightforward enough, so why are so many people blind-sided when Medicare stops paying the bills? In most cases, the trouble starts when the need arises for non-rehabilitative or custodial care services.

HYPOTHETICAL EXAMPLE

Medicare does not care about your long-term care.

Carol had no idea, as she called her husband Peter in for lunch, that her life was about to change forever. He was working outside in the garden, and after several attempts to get his attention without a response, she felt something must be wrong. As Carol walked outside, she saw that Peter was unable to talk and had lost the ability to move the right side of his body.

Peter was having a severe stroke. After three weeks in the hospital he began making some progress with acute care and rehabilitation therapy. At this point his doctor released him to a skilled nursing facility for additional treatment.

Carol's attitude was looking up as Peter was released from the hospital. She was sure Medicare would pay for the additional services he needed at the nursing home for 100 days, just as she had read in the materials she had been given.

What she didn't realize was that the 100 days of coverage started back in the skilled-care floor at the hospital. His remaining days of coverage were already numbered, yet after another four weeks, Peter's therapy sessions became increasingly difficult. He still needed help eating and bathing, but despite all the therapy and hard work, his progress toward accomplishing these tasks on his own was very limited.

Peter was frustrated and depressed, and Carol could do little to encourage her husband. At this point, the therapist and Peter's primary care doctor had a discussion. They agreed that Peter was showing no improvement, and the primary care doctor reported this to Medicare.

To Carol's dismay, she soon received word that Medicare would no longer be paying for Peter's care because he needed "custodial care" and Medicare only pays for 100 days of "skilled care." Carol didn't know what to do. She thought she had another couple of months to make a decision about his care and its financial implications. What was she going to do? How would she pay?

Most people already understand that hospitals will only keep you as long as they really need to. So what happens when you have to leave the hospital? Depending on where you go and what type of care you are receiving, the maximum amount of time that Medicare will continue to pay for rehab or recovery services is 100 days.

That's right, 100 days, and that is it. Even worse is the fact that many individuals receive far fewer than 100 days due to other loopholes in the Medicare system. This can have a chilling effect on a lot of people's warm, fuzzy feelings about Medicare and the stability it provided (up to this point).

IT HAPPENS ALL THE TIME.

Hundreds of thousands of families have experienced a similar situation. As long as patients are making progress as a result of their therapy, it is considered "skilled care" by Medicare and Medicare supplement insurance plans. Either can provide up to 100 days of skilled care, if needed, as long as the patient is making noticeable progress.

So what happens when progress ends and the person is still unable to perform routine activities of daily living, such as eating, bathing, or dressing?

Medicare can consider this type of care "custodial," which it doesn't cover. In addition, regarding "skilled care," Medicare can require a minimum hospital stay of three days before services will be covered.

What does this mean? It means paying $15 to $20 per hour for a home healthcare nurse, $3,000 to $5,000 per month for assisted living care, or $8,000-plus dollars per month for nursing home care.

Conditions such as Alzheimer's and Parkinson's are long-term degenerative disorders, and skilled care simply is not an option because rehabilitation is of little help. Sadly, many

---

Medicare simply does not have the resources to pay for long-term care, which can cost anywhere between $6,000 and $10,000-plus per month.

---

other conditions fall into this category, leaving an enormous number of people uncovered by Medicare for much-needed assistance.

I hope that reading this chapter will bring some clarity to the areas where our healthcare system really leaves you to fend for yourself. This problem will only increase due to longer life expectancies and health conditions that can be treated today that could not be treated in years past. You may live 10 years longer, but what will the quality of those 10 years be?

Medicare simply does not have the resources to pay for long-term care, which can cost anywhere between $6,000 and $10,000-plus per month. Medicare was never intended to be the piggy bank for this. (Many people confuse Medicare with Medicaid in how long-term care costs are covered. We'll discuss Medicaid in the next chapter.)

The key thing to remember here is not to rely on Medicare to pay for long-term care services. As you navigate your way to a financially secure retirement, assuming Medicare will cover long-term care is just an accident waiting to happen.

CHAPTER 2

MEDICAID MISCONCEPTIONS

*You've worked a lifetime to build
your income and other financial resources.
Now get ready for an abrupt U-turn as you
attempt to "spend down," or divest, these assets
so you'll qualify for Medicaid benefits.*

To reiterate, Medicare is health insurance, not long-term care insurance. So when Medicare cuts you off like a driver changing three lanes of traffic in front of you, what's the next link on the benefit chain? Medicaid, which can pay for nursing home care and even some in-home healthcare.

Here's the catch: You have to pass a strict income and asset test before Medicaid will pay one dime toward anything. In layman's terms, you have to be considered impoverished before this program will pay for your care.

Unlike Medicare, which is run at the federal level and has a uniform benefit structure, Medicaid is administered at the state level. Even though it is a federal program, each state can interpret Medicaid qualification rules differently, which can lead to conflicting and confusing decisions about eligibility.

In terms of qualifying for Medicaid, every state has three basic eligibility tests:

- *Category Test*–Applicants must be at least 65 years old, blind or disabled. For most seniors needing custodial or nursing home care services, meeting this requirement is no problem.

- *Income Test*–This determines how much of the patient's income will need to be "spent down" to the nursing home, typically all income minus a personal needs allowance (usually under $60 a month). Additional income rules are in place in certain states, called "income cap" states. This means if the applicant has an income greater than $2,022 a month they will be disqualified from Medicaid. (If this is the case, there are planning options that may allow eligibility under certain conditions.)

- *Asset Test*–This is how much Medicaid will allow you to keep. In most states this is $2,000 for an individual, or up to $109,560 for couples. Please note, for couples this represents the maximum of one-half of your combined countable assets. States will also allow a healthy spouse to keep a minimum of $21,912 for those who have limited assets.

This means that most middle- and upper middle-class families face major challenges spending down, or dispersing, their assets before Medicaid is even an option. On the brighter side, the rules are different for single applicants vs. married couples, and some resources are considered exempt – meaning that when you apply for Medicaid they are safe from having to be spent down. As you'll see ahead, this can be tricky.

WHAT YOU CAN KEEP

Your home (but don't count on it)
Whether you are single or married, your primary residence is considered exempt as long as you or your spouse continue to live in it. For example, if you are in a nursing home, your spouse can continue to live at home without having to sell the property. The same applies if you are single and receiving in-home custodial care.

This asset exemption only applies to the primary residence; any other property won't have the same benefits. Also, in most states, this rule applies only to the first $500,000 of equity in the house. Any equity beyond this can be considered countable in a spend-down situation. Certain states can use a higher amount of equity; but it is important to note, regardless of value, there can be some other tests that can change your home to a countable asset. (I told you this stuff is tricky!) Here are a couple of examples to illustrate.

Under current Medicaid laws, the state can and will be able to collect any amounts paid by Medicaid for your care through

---

This means that if the state has paid, say, $100,000 toward your care, it can put a lien for this amount on your home before it can go to your kids.

---

a process called estate recovery. What is the largest asset people have after they have spent down all their other assets to qualify for Medicaid? You guessed it, their home.

This means that if the state has paid, say, $100,000 toward your care, it can put a lien for this amount on your home before it can go to your kids. Most states also have expanded the definition of estate recovery to include life estates and assets held in a revocable living trust. When this happens, your beneficiaries will have to "settle up" with the state before they see any funds from the sale of the house.

Most states also have an "intent to return" rule that assumes the Medicaid applicant has the intention of returning home, regardless of the care services they're receiving. Some states, however, perform a subjective test to determine if the applicant really is coming home. In Virginia, they can use this test after Medicaid has paid the bills for six months. At this point, if they believe that coming home is not an option, they can consider the primary home a countable asset.

Medicaid will not come after you for your television or sofa, but don't try to get too slick on this.

Money from the sale of the home is not an exempt asset. This means that the painful spend-down process starts all over again with any proceeds from the home.

The government will not notify you of any of this. Never assume, if you are on Medicaid, that your house is a safe asset that will remain yours.

Personal belongings

Under most circumstances, items such as your clothes, jewelry and furniture are considered exempt assets. Medicaid will not come after you for your television or sofa, but don't try to get too slick on this.

If, say, you decide to purchase a $100,000 piece of artwork, this could be met with some resistance from the social worker who is working on your Medicaid claim.

The important thing to note here is that in most cases they will not come after belongings or personal effects that were not intended as collectibles.

Automobile

You are allowed one vehicle, regardless of value, as a means of transportation. The automobile must provide for the transportation of the Medicaid applicant or a household member of the family. I have seen people take advantage of this by purchasing expensive cars (often called "Medicaid Cadillacs").

This is perfectly legal, but the proof lies on you to show how the vehicle is being used. For example, a Ferrari could be considered a collectible if it isn't used according to Medicaid rules. In addition, as you'll see in Chapter 3, this wouldn't be a very efficient way to protect assets.

Life insurance and burial expenses

Certain life insurance policies allow the policy itself to be exempt. The most common of these are group policies that an employer owns while you are the insured party. These policies typically have no cash value to collect against. Term insurance policies have the benefit of accruing no cash value and therefore are also exempt.

The problem lies in any policy that has a value of over $1,500. Any cash values in policies that are greater than $1,500 will be considered a countable asset. For instance, if you took out a policy with a $100,000 face value and the policy has built up $15,000 in cash, this policy would be an available resource to pay for your care. If you have to use all of the cash in the policy, your policy most likely will lapse and you would lose the death benefit.

Even if you purchased a life policy to cover your funeral expenses, the same guidelines are used. A lot of individuals purchase small policies, but even if it's just for, say, $10,000, the same resource rules apply.

Medicaid does, however, give you the chance to pre-pay your burial expenses, for which most states allow $12,500. This needs to be done correctly, though. That means you have to set this up as irrevocable and unassignable as a pre-paid funeral contract. Make sure that you have this completed by someone who understands burial and funeral contracts and policies to keep things on the straight and narrow here.

WHAT YOU CAN'T KEEP

Anything beyond the items listed above are normally counted as spend-down assets before Medicaid kicks in. Your checking, savings, CDs, IRAs, stocks, bonds, most annuities, and properties beyond your primary residence are all countable assets. Bottom line: If you can spend it, so can they.

"OK, SO I'LL GIVE IT AWAY."

Sounds good, right? If you're already spending thousands of dollars a month for your care before the government will lift a finger to help, why not give away your assets to your children,

---

In all states, Medicaid has what is called a "look-back" period that applies to any gifts made in the last 60 months.

---

church, or other charities? After the assets are gone, Medicaid will step in and start footing the bill, right?

Wrong.

In all states, Medicaid has what is called a "look-back" period that applies to any gifts made in the last 60 months. It is important to note here when the penalty begins, because the rules changed drastically when Congress passed the Deficit Reduction Act (DRA) of 2005.

How the penalty is applied is the "gotcha" here, because it is not when the gift is made, but when your Medicaid application is filed. For example, say you gave your granddaughter $50,000 toward her education. Under the pre-DRA rules, the penalty period would have started as of the date you gave it to her. They would divide this $50,000 into a monthly penalty divisor of the cost of care in the area you live. If that amount was $5,000 per month, you would have to wait 10 months to qualify for Medicaid under the old rules, provided all other assets were used and you were below the asset level needed to qualify for Medicaid.

Not so today. After the DRA, the penalty period does not start until the Medicaid application is submitted. You could be healthy, but 52 months later have a stroke and need nursing home care, just like Peter in Chapter 1. Four years later, for example, you have used all your other assets, so now you submit an application for Medicaid benefits because you're broke.

How the penalty is applied is the "gotcha" here, because it is not when the gift is made, but when your Medicaid application is filed.

Guess what? The same 10-month penalty period does not begin until your Medicaid application is submitted. This is a huge problem. Who will pay for the 10 months of care? What happens when the nursing home needs payment and no one is paying the bill?

This is a sticky situation, to say the least. Hey, maybe your

---

*OK, pay close attention here: Adding a son or daughter's name to your account(s) will offer you **no** advantages toward Medicaid eligibility, and it can cause other problems that you may not be aware of.*

---

granddaughter will move in and take care of you for the 10 months before Medicaid kicks in… What do you think?

MORE BUMPS IN THE ROAD

Even if you get through the 60-month look-back period, other problems can arise when "gifting," or adding a son or daughter's name to your accounts.

OK, pay close attention here: Adding a son or daughter's name to your account(s) will offer you *no* advantages toward Medicaid eligibility, and it can cause other problems that you may not be aware of.

Say you add your son's name to your accounts, and he gets in a car accident and is sued for everything he has, including your money that has his name on it. His divorce or other financial issues could come into play in the same way.

I'm sure the last thing you want is a daughter or son-in-law

I'm sure the last thing you want is a daughter or son-in-law fighting for half of your money that isn't theirs. I hate to say it, but this stuff does happen. It's called the kids' problems "bumping into" your money.

---

fighting for half of your money that isn't theirs. I hate to say it, but this stuff does happen. It's called the kids' problems "bumping into" your money.

You probably have the best intentions by adding an adult child's name to your accounts or gifting money to your kids. Just make sure you know the pitfalls in titling or transferring assets directly to them. There are other avenues to protect you from these kinds of problems, as you will soon see.

CHAPTER 3

MAKING CENTS OF YOUR HEALTHCARE OPTIONS

```
TOLL
BOOTH
AHEAD
```

Fifty percent of Americans over 65 will need long-term care (LTC) services, and even those with LTC insurance may wind up with substantial out-of-pocket costs. Know your options. Plan smart. **Plan now.**

No one could have reasonably foreseen what disarray our healthcare system would be in today. For seniors and retirees, I can only express the importance of putting up a financial fight now, not later. Planning now can give you a path to the security that you want during your retirement years. This chapter will look at several options and how each may or may not help protect your assets from the devastating costs of long-term care.

LONG-TERM CARE INSURANCE

Long-term care (LTC) insurance was introduced in the 1970s and originally paid for nursing home care. Policies now can cover numerous care options as well as pay different benefits based on policy provisions.

Yet today there are some troubling trends in LTC insurance that could change how policyholders and potential buyers view this coverage.

Insurance companies pay millions of dollars in claims every year toward custodial and other long-term care services. I have seen many instances in which LTC insurance was the only thing keeping families afloat while paying for care. Yet today there are some troubling trends in LTC insurance that could change how policyholders and potential buyers view this coverage. For example:

Rate hikes

Over the past couple of years, I have seen many companies raise policyholders' rates—as much as 50% in some cases.

Most LTC policies have provisions that allow the insurance company to raise rates based on the claim history and other financial factors.

For policyholders who are on a fixed income during retirement, an increase of 20% or more could cause a financial hardship when covering all other monthly expenses. After having their policy for 10 to 15 years, some policyholders are forced to drop the coverage because they can no longer afford the premiums. Talk about money down the drain!

This is something you need to plan for when looking at

The medical inflation rate is far outpacing the inflation rate that most LTC insurance coverers calculate into their policies.

LTC insurance. Stay alert and know that most companies are looking to increase rates in the future due to higher than expected claims and lower investment returns.

Partial coverage

In addition to potential rate hikes, pay attention to the basic economics of long-term care. The medical inflation rate is far outpacing the inflation rate that most LTC insurance coverers calculate into their policies. Inflation protection in LTC policies generally ranges from 3% to 5% with an option to choose. While this is good to cover *additional* LTC costs, keep in mind that the rate of nursing home charges has basically doubled over the past 10 years.

If you took out a policy 10 years ago, the costs may have been $100 a day for skilled nursing care. Now the same care is averaging over $200 a day. Your policy with inflation protection of 5% would lag by some $40 a day. This would be $1,200 or more a month out of your pocket—costs you may have assumed would be covered when you purchased the LTC policy.

It is important to add that LTC insurance can definitely be of help with planning for care expenses, just know this is not going to be the "end all, be all" for your LTC planning needs.

SPECIFIC LONG-TERM CARE INSURANCE

OPTIONS FOR SPECIFIC NEEDS

It's not all bad news on the LTC insurance front. Over the past several years we've seen several new coverage options offering solid benefits. For example:

Partnership protection provision

One thing that does help with LTC policies is that most states now have something called partnership protection. If you ever use all of your policy benefits, this provision allows you to apply for Medicaid and keep, dollar-for-dollar, the amount used in the policy without having to spend it down to qualify.

Asset-based LTC allows the insured to carry income tax-free life insurance that can also be used for long-term care, if needed.

This can allow you to protect more of your money for your family if or when long-term care services are needed. Not all policies have this provision, so you'll need to find a company that offers this type of coverage in your state.

Asset-based LTC

In my office, we like to use a specific type of coverage called asset-based LTC, which helps people avoid some of the traditional LTC insurance pitfalls. It differs from traditional, or standalone, LTC insurance and can offer a solution to the problems previously outlined.

Asset-based LTC allows the insured to carry income tax-free life insurance that can also be used for long-term care, if needed. This strategy eliminates the threat of rate increases and allows policyholders to provide money to their beneficiaries if the policy is not used for long-term care.

The policies are not experienced rated, so this new breed of

This strategy eliminates the threat of rate increases and allows policyholders to provide money to their beneficiaries if the policy is not used for long-term care.

---

coverage does not have surprise rate increases down the road. By estimating life expectancy and cost of care, it can financially benefit a family to purchase this type of coverage up front, knowing the money will either go to pay for care, if needed, or to your spouse or kids if you don't use it. This can be particularly beneficial to the family, since the insurance benefits paid at death are income tax-free.

The money you put into a plan for covering long-term care for you or a spouse can protect both of you, so *please plan now.* For healthy or moderately healthy individuals, asset-based LTC is an option worth considering. I recommend that you work with an experienced planner who thoroughly understands your family's financial picture as well as the intricacies of today's LTC insurance policies.

GIFTS AND TRUSTS:

How you give can be more important than *what* you give.

Using an irrevocable, or "hybrid," trust can provide asset protection from future long-term care costs as well as help avert the potential family problems raised in Chapter 2.

Properly drafted, an irrevocable trust enables completed gifts to family members without exposing the money to their

---

Properly drafted, an irrevocable trust enables completed gifts to family members without exposing the money to their creditors or creating large capital gains taxes.

---

creditors or creating large capital gains taxes. Gifted funds can also be set up to be tax-deferred until needed to provide additional growth opportunity inside the specialized trust.

As you will read in Chapters 4 through 6, not all trust documents—or legal documents in general—are created equal. Building a legal foundation that provides flexibility and asset protection is a must if you plan to succeed during these uncertain economic times.

CHAPTER 4

IS YOUR POWER OF ATTORNEY POWERLESS?

PROCEED
WITH
CAUTION

A simple oversight can take away, rather than give, the power to protect your assets. Make sure your power of attorney (POA) speaks for your future self in case you can't.

Among the problems we see every day in our office are clients' legal documents that do not address options that may be available if a long-term disability strikes someone in their family. This does not mean that their will, trust and supporting documents (such as a power of attorney and living will) were done improperly. More than likely, the documents address what should happen to their assets when they die, not what should happen if they become incapacitated and need skilled facility care.

With life expectancies consistently on the rise, the new question is: What happens to all of the assets you have accumulated if you live for years and need long-term care? At the cost of $7,000 or more per month for skilled nursing facility care in our area, this problem should no longer be ignored.

You are probably asking, "What does this have to do with my power of attorney?" We're getting there, but first let's make

---

A financial or general durable POA can be a powerful document if you are no longer able to manage your affairs. This document should allow someone you appoint (your "agent") to make decisions about your everyday financial affairs, including important financial decisions.

---

sure you know the importance of having a properly drafted power of attorney (POA) that has been signed and notarized.

A POA is usually drawn up as a supporting document to your will or trust planning. Don't assume it's just a bunch of legalese. A financial or general durable POA can be a powerful document if you are no longer able to manage your affairs. This document should allow someone you appoint (your "agent") to make decisions about your everyday financial affairs, including important financial decisions.

What happens if you have a stroke or are diagnosed with dementia? You guessed it, the agent appointed in your POA may only perform the duties that are set forth in the document you executed.

BE CAREFUL WHAT YOU ASK FOR.

A common concern today is whether or not the agent you specify will take advantage of you if you need help tending to your finances because of mental and/or physical incapacity. Because of this, many well-intentioned attorneys add restrictive language regarding gifting in order to prevent agents from making excessive gifts to themselves or others.

A common clause meant to stem this problem may read something like this:

"I permit my agent to make gifts on my behalf. However, this gift may not exceed the IRS annual gift exclusion amount allowed during any calendar year."

The IRS annual gift exclusion rule allows people to gift up to a certain amount per year, per person, without it being counted toward their one-time, lifetime gifting exclusion amount. In 2010, the annual gift exclusion amount was $13,000.

Though inserted for your protection, the POA language above can cause you to lose assets you might need if a long-term disability occurs that requires skilled nursing care—assets that could be protected if the POA was drafted differently.

Say you have worked hard and saved $400,000 in your retirement account, and then you are diagnosed with Alzheimer's. What happens when you can no longer make your own financial decisions?

For example, many retirees today receive Social Security and some form of retirement plan (IRA, 401k, etc.) distributions that they use to supplement their monthly income. Most retirees have been making contributions to their retirement accounts for 30 to 40 years. This type of account is individually owned, which means that the holder's spouse or children cannot be joint owners without triggering substantial income tax consequences. Even though the spouse and/or children may be beneficiaries, only the individual owner has the right to access this money directly.

Say you have worked hard and saved $400,000 in your retirement account, and then you are diagnosed with Alzheimer's. What happens when you can no longer make your own financial decisions? If the designated agent under your POA is your spouse or a child, what have you permitted them to do under the provisions of your POA?

What if your agent had the ability to protect this money from all being spent down on skilled nursing home care? Even if they are advised that they could do so by transferring the ownership of the funds out of your individual name, they would only be able to move $13,000 per year out of your individual account while paying the nursing home $70,000 to $80,000 per year.

Unlimited gifting may allow for additional asset protection planning on your individual retirement account for the benefit of your family.

HOW TO DO IT RIGHT

Do yourself and your family a favor by familiarizing yourself with the language in all of your legal documents, beginning with your POA. Does it include limited gifting language? If so, you might want to re-think that.

Do you even have a valid POA?

If you don't, I urge you to have one drawn up with the help of an experienced elder and estate planning attorney who is educated in disability planning. In the absence of a properly prepared POA, the court will have to get involved and may become your decision maker regarding the spend-down of your assets.

CHAPTER 5

THE "I LOVE YOU, BUT..." WILL

You don't want a nursing home to be the beneficiary of your estate, right? Unfortunately, that may be exactly what happens if you aren't prepared for a disability within the family.

A last will and testament is a legal document used by most individuals as a means of instructing executors how to distribute their assets at death. Many couples use traditional "I Love You" wills to direct their assets' distribution.

What is the "I Love You" will?

It's a basic will directing that when you die, all of your just debts and expenses be paid, then the remainder of your estate goes to your spouse. If your spouse dies first, then the remaining assets go to your children. Your spouse's will contains the same language. If you predecease your spouse, your estate will be distributed to your children. Your spouse is named as executor, and then a child may be named as successor executor.

There is nothing wrong with an "I Love You" plan, so long as you or your spouse never get sick and need care. But keep in mind that a will has to be probated. If your goal is to have

---

If your goal is to have things run quickly and smoothly, probate may not always be the best answer. It can become time consuming and expensive, particularly if there are complications administering your estate.

---

things run quickly and smoothly, probate may not always be the best answer. It can become time consuming and expensive, particularly if there are complications administering your estate.

When you die, your executor takes the will to be recorded at the circuit court where you last resided and submits an inventory of your assets.

This can trigger a series of circumstances that can have a dramatic impact on what is actually inherited by your loved ones:

- *First, the contents of your will become public record.* This can trigger disputes among family members and provide notification to creditors eager to take their share of your assets.

- *Second, the cost of probate itself can be very expensive,* depending on the value of your probate estate.

- *Third, and perhaps most problematic, is that 50% of families include someone who will need some type of long-term care.* As you learned in Chapter 1, the costs of long-term care can soar to $10,000+ a month, and Medicaid won't be a viable resource for your long-term care costs until all of your assets are depleted. That means your entire estate can be wiped out by the costs of a nursing home, assisted living, or even in-home healthcare.

Let's see what might happen if the attorney for Peter and Carol from Chapter 1 had drafted "I Love You" wills for their estate plan.

Peter is now in a nursing home and Carol is writing checks monthly to pay for his care. Each and every month Carol has the mounting stress of taking care of the household bills and paying Peter's medical bills, plus troublesome concerns about what level of care her husband may need for the rest of his life. While everyone is focused on Peter's medical care and condition, the stress weighs heavily on Carol. Even though she

---

Do you think this is what Peter and Carol wanted—all of their hard-earned money to go to the nursing home? Of course not. They would have wanted their children and grandchildren to have what was left.

---

is considered the "healthy" spouse, guess what happens…Carol dies first!

Remember the "I Love You" provisions in the will? Even if Carol wanted the children to inherit her assets, her will states all she owns be distributed to Peter. Where is he? In a nursing home. Where does the money go now? It goes to Peter, who needs thousands of dollars of care per month. His money (and

Carol's) will have to be spent down to under $2,000 dollars before the government will step in to help cover the exorbitant monthly bill. In the end there will be nothing left.

Do you think this is what Peter and Carol wanted—all of their hard-earned money to go to the nursing home? Of course not. They would have wanted their children and grandchildren to have what was left.

The attorney who drafted the "I Love You" wills did nothing wrong. Like most people—maybe even you—Peter and Carol weren't thinking about long-term care when they drafted their wills, they were thinking about what happens when you die. Today, you have to think about both.

How do you address disability planning in addition to death planning in your estate? I urge families to consider the "I Love You, But…" estate plan. This means that if one spouse dies and the other needs long-term care, the assets are directed to a specialized trust. This allows Medicaid to step in sooner and your assets to pass to your children, not the nursing home.

CHAPTER 6

THE REVOCABLE LIVING TRUST

AVOID
BLIND
SPOTS

While removing a number of estate planning roadblocks, the revocable living trust can still leave a blind spot when it comes to disability planning.

As you read in the previous chapter, most estate plans revolve around a last will and testament, which requires probating the estate. There is a way to avoid all of this, however, and that is through a revocable living trust. If properly funded (which means assets titled or beneficiaried to your trust), the revocable living trust circumvents the need for probate and enables you to maintain control of your assets while you're living, and to specifically direct your successor, or "trustee," with regard to the distribution of your assets after your incapacity and/or death.

A revocable living trust is a private contract between:

- *The grantor*–The person who establishes the trust.
- *The trustee*–The person who controls the trust assets.

- *The beneficiary, or beneficiaries*–Those who benefit from the income and principal of the trust.

Most individuals favor this type of trust because they are able to maintain total control over their assets while they are living and are competent. In addition, most living trusts are identified by the grantor's Social Security number, so no additional tax reporting is necessary when managing the assets inside the trust.

Here's an example of how a family could use a revocable living trust to their benefit:

JOHN AND CLAIRE EXECUTED REVOCABLE LIVING TRUSTS and directed their assets into the "John Living Trust" and the "Claire Living Trust." They liked the fact that as trustees of their own trusts, they could leave money to their son Warren and not worry about their estates having to go through probate and information about their assets being entered into the public record. Also, John and Claire may make changes or amend their trusts at any time, so long as they remain legally competent. They may change the beneficiaries, spend any or all amounts in the trust, or even revoke their respective trust.

During their lifetimes, John and Claire accumulated over $500,000 in savings and investments. These assets were moved inside their trusts along with their home, all of which would avoid probate. Several years later, John passed away and Claire was left to manage all of the trust assets. As she grew older, she was diagnosed with dementia and was no longer able to manage the affairs of the trust. Thankfully, Warren is very responsible. John and Claire set their trusts up to name him as a successor trustee in the event that either of them were unable to serve as trustee. This is another advantage to living trust planning in the event of disability instead of death.

HERE'S WHERE YOU CAN RUN INTO TROUBLE

Warren was the successor trustee, and he stepped up to act in the capacity of trustee when his mom was diagnosed with dementia and was therefore incapacitated.

If your trust includes language referred to as "HEMS" provisions, which are very common, it could be a problem.

Remember that John and Claire could make amendments to the trust provisions when they were serving as trustee and had their full mental and physical capacities.

Once Warren steps up as the successor trustee, he cannot change the trust provisions. He is required to follow the terms of the trust and faces potential civil liability for violating any of his fiduciary responsibilities as trustee if he deviates from those provisions.

Why could this be a problem? If your trust includes language referred to as "HEMS" provisions, which are very common, it could be a problem. HEMS stands for health, education, maintenance and support. Warren is required to use the funds in the trust to take care of his mother's health. What happens if she is in a nursing home? According to the trust, Warren must use the trust funds for Claire's health. So where do the trust funds go? To the nursing home. Once these types

---

Revocable trusts by design are not created for asset protection planning when dealing with a disability or a financial spend-down. Medicaid makes it clear that if you have access to your money directly, they can and most likely will tell you to spend it on your long-term care.

---

of distributions begin, it may be impossible to protect any of the trust assets from being spent down to the nursing home.

Revocable trusts by design are not created for asset protection planning when dealing with a disability or a financial spend-down. Medicaid makes it clear that if you have access to your money directly, they can and most likely will tell you to spend it on your long-term care.

If you are considering a trust when developing your estate plan, make sure to build in the flexibility for financial options that could protect your money from being directed to a nursing home or spent down on medical needs that may arise in the future. Consult a financial and legal planning team to help you structure a trust that takes disability planning into consideration as well as other essential factors in determining where your assets go during your life as well as after you are incapacitated or deceased.

CHAPTER 7

THE SOCIAL SECURITY
AND PENSION SHUFFLE

When a spouse dies, the surviving partner may be forced into a sharp financial turn for the worse. Avoid this unwanted change of course with an "income then inheritance" trust plan.

Social Security is central to the successful, stable retirement of many seniors, and extended life expectancies made this benefit more important than ever. Did you know that for every two 65-year-olds, there's a 45% chance that one will live to age 90 or older?[2] Beyond coping with the loss of a loved one, the surviving spouse often faces serious financial dilemmas, particularly in relation to pensions and other retirement assets.

Let's use James and Elizabeth as a hypothetical example. James retired after working 35 years at the nearby plant.

---

[2]Center of Medicare and Medicaid Services, publication #11306

Elizabeth was a homemaker who raised two beautiful daughters. She went back to work after they were grown.

They both started Social Security when Jim retired at 65, and at that time he also began collecting a straight pension from his former employer. Jim and Elizabeth were good savers, and everything was paid for, including their house with no debt. With $4,500 a month in retirement income, things were good (see Financial Snapshot 1, below). They were able to travel, go out for dinner, and have the comfortable lifestyle that they always wanted for their retirement years.

FINANCIAL SNAPSHOT 1

MONTHLY INCOME	James	Elizabeth	Total
Social Security	$1,800	$1,000	$2,800
Pension	$1,700		$1,700
Total Monthly Income			$4,500

RETIREMENT SAVINGS	James	Elizabeth	Total
			$400,000

All was good for James and Elizabeth until… James died. At that point, the financial landscape changed considerably for Elizabeth (see Financial Snapshot 2, below).

FINANCIAL SNAPSHOT 2

MONTHLY INCOME	James	Elizabeth	Total
Social Security	~~$1,800~~	~~$1,000~~ $1,800	$1,800
Pension	~~$1,700~~		
Total Monthly Income			$1,800

As you can see, Elizabeth's Social Security benefit was replaced by James' higher payment, but his monthly pension distribution was lost because it was a "straight" pension account that dies with the holder. Elizabeth's monthly income was slashed to $1,800 from $4,500, a whopping 60% less. She can't begin to maintain her former standard of living. In our office we call this situation "moving to a new neighborhood"–and not a good one!

You're probably thinking, "Hey, wait a minute, that's why they saved $400,000 for retirement. Elizabeth can use the interest from that to offset the loss of income." True, that would allow her to make up for most, if not all, of the difference. But what happens if James needed nursing home care before he died? Do you think the $400,000 would still be there in its entirety for Elizabeth?

Reduced Social Security and pension payments leave many surviving spouses with a drastically smaller income.

Reduced Social Security and pension payments leave many surviving spouses with a drastically smaller income. Combined with a loss of retirement assets due to long-term care, inflation and market losses, all too many retirees become stuck in a financial "neighborhood" they never imagined for themselves.

To circumvent this situation, our office utilizes a strategy called "income then inheritance" trust planning. The success of this plan is derived from a very specific trust document paired with financial and insurance products to replenish lost income for the spouse.

Here's how it works. Say James is now 68, with a life expectancy of 17 years. How much money do we need to put away today for his wife to receive the $2,700 dollars of lost income when he dies? This is calculated using a formula to determine the amount of money that needs to be invested today to allow enough money to generate exactly $2,700 a month for Elizabeth in the future. (In this case, if James is in poor health,

---

Combined with a loss of retirement assets due to long-term care, inflation and market losses, all too many retirees become stuck in a financial "neighborhood" they never imagined for themselves.

---

we adjust the life expectancy accordingly.)

To carry out James' wishes, we want to protect his wife's future income as well as the value of the rest of their estate to pass on to their daughters. The trust document can execute this arrangement if drafted properly, plus allow for increased protection from nursing home costs if either James or Elizabeth's health fails. This is why we call this "income then inheritance" planning.

It is imperative that you work with an experienced legal and financial team to achieve this goal. You must have properly titled beneficiaries and language specific to asset protection planning within the trust. Executed correctly, this is a powerful way to protect income and assets for your spouse and children.

CHAPTER 8

MAPPING YOUR SUCCESSFUL RETIREMENT

*Believe it or not, you **can** gain peace of mind about your financial resources for retirement. Here's how.*

Wen should I start Social Security? What options should I choose if I have a pension? How should I invest my money so I can feel secure for the rest of my life? These are the questions I hear most often when I'm helping people develop their retirement plans—which sometimes happens even after people have retired, because a solid financial foundation was never established to begin with.

Many of you have been pitched different investments without so much as an overview of what your goals are. How can you sign off on a financial decision concerning your retirement when specific goals have not even been addressed?

This chapter is dedicated to building a financial foundation for anyone who is near retirement or already retired.

The process I use is called CPR, which stands for *complete planning review.* Going through the steps shown in the diagram

CPR | COMPLETE PLA

INVESTMENT
CENTS
"GROWING YOUR
NUMBER"

ESTATE AND INC
PRESERVATIO
"PROTECTING YOUR

FOUNDATION INCOME
"KNOWING YOUR N

A TRUE TE

below provides clear direction on how to prioritize your goals and stresses the importance of comprehensive planning.

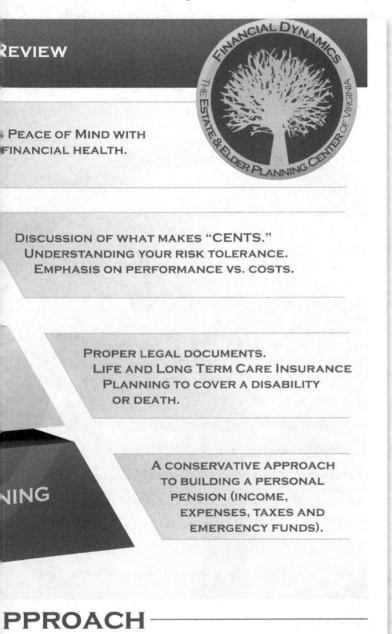

REVIEW

PEACE OF MIND WITH
FINANCIAL HEALTH.

DISCUSSION OF WHAT MAKES "CENTS."
UNDERSTANDING YOUR RISK TOLERANCE.
EMPHASIS ON PERFORMANCE VS. COSTS.

PROPER LEGAL DOCUMENTS.
LIFE AND LONG TERM CARE INSURANCE
PLANNING TO COVER A DISABILITY
OR DEATH.

A CONSERVATIVE APPROACH
TO BUILDING A PERSONAL
PENSION (INCOME,
EXPENSES, TAXES AND
EMERGENCY FUNDS).

NING

PPROACH

We start with a process called foundation income planning. This is the need to first and foremost establish what your budget is and consider what it may be in the future. The need for reliable monthly income is paramount for today's retiree.

We start with a process called foundation income planning. This is the need to first and foremost establish what your budget is and consider what it may be in the future.

Social Security is miserably falling behind inflation. (If you don't believe me, look at the cost of your health insurance or the price of gasoline. Has your Social Security increased enough to cover these expenses?) Even if you have a pension, most families have underestimated what the actual costs of living are and will be. In addition, most retirees have not considered expenses, such as taxes and fees, on any sources of supplemental income.

This is all part of the foundation, and it has to be addressed first to establish a stable retirement. This means having a conservative approach with this portion of your retirement assets. Time is simply not on your side when you lose money, especially when you are using it for income. I define conservative as trying to minimize risk with income that can be depended

---

Interest rates have made this a tough go for retirees looking for income from CDs, bonds, and fixed annuities, but the annuity by far has been the silver lining for those who want dependable income.

---

on. Interest rates have made this a tough go for retirees looking for income from CDs, bonds, and fixed annuities, but the annuity by far has been the silver lining for those who want dependable income[3].

Someone, somewhere started the whole "annuities are bad" kick. What a disservice this has been to today's retirees! I'm not a fan of all annuities; and, yes, just like all invest-

---

[3] Insurance product guarantees are subject to the claims-paying ability of the issuing company.

ments, there are pros and cons. Yet a properly placed annuity can guarantee an income stream for the life of the individual or couple. I know of no other investment that can offer that kind of guarantee. With the recent market meltdowns, even the government has been looking into annuities as a way to help with retirement income. I have seen too many families feel the wrath of huge swings in the market with money they

---

During retirement, you may

never be able to get back

what you lose because time

is no longer on your side.

---

really need now, not later. Just make sure that you work with an advisor who understands this risk and knows that you simply cannot afford to outlive the money that is set aside for your retirement income.

Income from other sources, such as dividends and bonds, can also help. But remember, this involves greater risk. I personally have witnessed several retirees who depended on dividends from their stocks, thinking nothing would ever happen to those dividends. Well, we all know how that went during 2008 and early 2009. Not only did many companies (including banks) cut dividends, but the price of their stocks tumbled in value as well. During retirement, you may never be able to get back what you lose because time is no longer on your side.

Once you've added together your fixed and discretionary income needs (I call this "knowing your number"), then you can begin to have a discussion of what is needed for

---

Once you've added together your fixed and discretionary income needs (I call this "knowing your number"), then you can begin to have a discussion of what is needed for family protection.

---

family protection. Goals such as distributing your assets to your family, long-term care planning, and life insurance can be discussed during this part of the planning process. This equally important step is designed to protect your family's income due to death or disability. As you learned in previous chapters, income and assets can change dramatically when long-term care is needed or if a spouse passes away.

Legal documents should be reviewed and updated if necessary to facilitate proper distribution of your estate. Chapters 4 through 6 covered a lot of what should be discussed

---

Some people try to piecemeal a plan together with a bank here, a brokerage firm there, an insurance salesman at another company, and so on. This can result in a great deal of confusion, inefficiency and misdirected money, and in the end usually misses the mark entirely in terms of attaining retirement goals.

---

during this step. Remember, though, not all legal documents are created equal. I strongly recommend that you use an experienced estate and elder planning attorney as your guide during this process.

The next step in our CPR process is what I call investment "cents." This is where we walk clients through the true costs of all of their investments. Fees, both known and unknown, can wreak havoc on investment returns, so this step is critical in keeping costs at a minimum so you can hang on to as much of your money as possible. As you will read in the next chapter, investments such as mutual funds and variable annuities that use mutual fund clones, called subaccounts, can have fees that can truly zap performance.

Each CPR step is truly unique and important to mapping out a successful retirement. In our office, we go through all of the steps, listening carefully and making sure that our clients understand and believe in the plan we're developing together.

Some people try to piecemeal a plan together with a bank here, a brokerage firm there, an insurance salesman at another company, and so on. This can result in a great deal of confusion, inefficiency and misdirected money, and in the end usually misses the mark entirely in terms of attaining retirement goals.

I urge you to consider working with a retirement planning professional—or close-knit team of professionals—to articulate your financial retirement goals and coordinate all aspects of achieving them.

CHAPTER 9

WATCH OUT FOR HIDDEN FEES

Ouch! Tired of getting hit by all those fine print fees in mutual funds? You might prefer a separately managed account (SMA), which gives you more control of your investment dollar.

In today's economic climate, it is no surprise that people look for ways to diversify investments of their hard-earned money. For years this has been accomplished with an investment vehicle known as a mutual fund. One benefit of a mutual fund is that it allows investors to buy into many different securities (i.e. stocks and bonds) to offer diversification. At its core, this has been the overriding benefit of mutual fund investing for over 30 years.

Over the past few years, savvy investors have started paying more attention to the costs associated with owning different types of mutual funds. When you purchase a mutual fund, either through your broker, advisor, through an employee savings plan, or if you simply do it yourself, you will receive a prospectus that discloses the fees associated with the fund. The problem is, the prospectus can be longer than this book. How many people have time to read page after page of prospectus reports? The last thing you need is a bunch of "fine print" fees when the stock market itself has basically been a roller coaster ride for the last 10 years! Don't underestimate the impact of these fees. Consider this example from the U.S. Department of Labor concerning fees within 401(k) plans (which are typically heavily weighted toward mutual fund investing):

> *"Assume that you are an employee with 35 years until retirement and a current 401(k) account balance of $25,000. If returns on investments in your account over the next 35 years average 7% and fees and expenses reduce your average returns by .5%, your account balance will grow to $227,000 at retirement, even if there are no further contributions to your account. If fees and expenses are 1.5%, however, your account balance will grow to only $163,000. The 1% difference in fees and expenses would reduce your account balance at retirement by 28%."* [4]

Let's go over what to pay particular attention to if you own mutual funds inside your investment portfolio. The first

---

[4] U.S. Department of Labor: http://www.dol.gov/ebsa/publications/401k_employee.html

distinction you should be aware of is the difference between "no-load" and "load" funds.

No-load funds are sold directly from mutual fund companies or financial "supermarkets" offering a wide range of investment products. Touted for "eliminating the middleman"

Just as people miss much of the fine print regarding mutual fund fees, a number of people don't have the time or investment knowledge to thoroughly research and understand the risks associated with the funds they're buying into.

—the financial advisor or broker—no-load funds come in all shapes, sizes, structures and performance levels.

Most funds purchased directly from the mutual fund company do not have any fees attached. These are called "true no-loads." When purchased from a financial supermarket, however, the majority of no-load funds incur 12b-1 fees, also known as the "cost of distribution." If these fees amount to more than .25% of the fund's average annual assets, the fund cannot be sold as a "no-load" product.

You might be saying to yourself that no-load mutual funds sound like a pretty good deal. On one hand, yes, they have helped many an investor get started with a regular savings plan. This has largely been the case with no-load mutual fund investments made through employee 401(k)s, for example.

On the other hand, scores of investors have, in hindsight,

Long story short, "eliminating the middleman" can often cost you money rather than save it.

---

wished they had worked with a financial advisor rather than getting involved with no-load funds. Just as people miss much of the fine print regarding mutual fund fees, a number of people don't have the time or investment knowledge to thoroughly research and understand the risks associated with the funds they're buying into.

Even worse, if a fund's performance tapers off – as frequently has been the case in recent years – most novice investors will sell it at exactly the wrong time! Long story short, "eliminating the middleman" can often cost you money rather than save it.

Load funds are typically are divided into three share types: "A" shares, "B" shares, and "C" shares. Each share class has a fee structure that can either help or hurt a mutual fund investor.

- *"A" shares* generally favor long-term investors who are willing to pay higher fees up front for lower fees in the long run. The deduction of these "front end" charges means that part of your money is not being invested. This share class is often used by investors who are willing to invest higher amounts into the fund or fund company, because the front-end fees may be discounted if the money invested meets a designated dollar amount, called a "breakpoint." An additional asset-based sales charge may also be applied annually, but it is typically lower than such charges on "B" and "C" shares. In the long run, if you buy and hold the mutual fund, this can be the most advantageous way to keep your costs lower than with other share classes.

- *"B" shares* remove the up-front fees and defer sales charges for the mutual fund investor. But this share class is riddled with higher annual or ongoing fees, and you may pay an additional sales charge or fee if you do not hold your money in the fund for a lengthy period of time. This type of fund also has come under attack for high 12b-1 fees, which are not required to cap at .25% as they are in no-load funds. There is no free lunch with this share class, and often a broker will position this as a no-load fund, so be careful. "B" shares have a less than stellar reputation because of these issues. If you see the letter B after your fund, you may want to ask the person who sold you the mutual fund to explain why.

- *"C" shares* typically charge an additional annual fee instead of front- or back-end sales charges. This is helpful for someone who feels they will be investing in the fund only for a short time. "C" shares can carry higher management fees, which can add up significantly over time. They have also come under scrutiny for being positioned as no-load funds if fees are at certain levels. Again, a 12b-1 fee can be attached here, and this can also eat away at returns. Also, some "C" shares will ding you with another fee if you cash out early – typically within 12 months – so stay alert here as well.

BUT WAIT, THERE'S MORE (FEES, THAT IS).

There are a lot of different cost structures to mutual funds, but at least my prospectus discloses all of this to me right? Not so fast… In addition to the confusion ensuing from lengthy prospectus reports, load- vs. no-load funds and complicated share classes, mutual funds can also harbor hidden fees, or trading costs. The expense of buying and selling the securities within the mutual fund can go unreported and usually are left to the mutual fund holder to piece together. If you are saying, "No big deal," you need to think again.

A recent study found these hidden fees averaged .66% and negatively impacted performance of the top 100 U.S. stock funds[5]. The problem is, no one is being held responsible for the disclosure of these fees in a clear and meaningful way. Paying too much in fees is a financial roadblock that everyone needs to address when planning for retirement, regardless of stock performance.

MORE CONTROL, MORE TRANSPARENCY

So what can you do? A separately managed account (SMA) may be an option worth considering. SMAs differ from mutual funds because the investor directly owns the investment rather than owning a share in a pool of investments. This can provide transparency and give you added control of your investment dollar.

An SMA allows you direct access to an investment team that can purchase stocks and other investments for you based on your goals. Since you actually own the investments yourself, you can usually can go online and understand exactly what you own in your portfolio, unlike a mutual fund that does not offer this kind of information access. In addition, you may be able

---

[5] *The Wall Street Journal,* "The Hidden Costs of Mutual Funds," 3-1-2010

to control when you buy and sell investments, which can offer tax advantages.

The reason most investors have not heard or participated in this type of account is that it was only an option for wealthy investors until recently. It was common to need a six-figure or

---

An SMA allows you direct

access to an investment team

that can purchase stocks

and other investments for

you based on your goals.

---

higher account balance before this option would be available due to the cost of setting up the portfolio. With low-cost trading platforms and products like exchange-traded funds (ETFs), separately managed accounts are now being used by many to improve performance and lower fees.

I have seen managed portfolios for well under $100,000, and some for as little as $25,000. SMAs have had a huge rise in investment dollars because of the clarity and costs compared to mutual funds.

If you have been saving through a 401(k) plan at work and are near retirement, it's worth asking your plan administrator if you're eligible for an "in-service" rollover. This would enable you to shift your money from high fee-incurring plans to other

---

The key here is to have an investment plan that allows you to understand all of your fees before investing. Make sure that someone makes a point of disclosing your fees before investing.

---

investments, an SMA for example, which could prove to be an extremely valuable change in the long run.

The key here is to have an investment plan that allows you to understand all of your fees before investing. Make sure that someone makes a point of disclosing your fees before investing. If someone is telling you about all of the benefits without any strings attached, a red flag should go up. All investments have pros and cons.

If this chapter helps you save 1% to 2% a year in fees, that may mean thousands of dollars more in your pocket during your retirement years...when you need it the most!

CHAPTER 10

WHERE TO GO FROM HERE

Why make the trip by yourself? Merging
with an experienced team is the best way to
reach your optimal retirement destination.

We've covered a lot of ground in this book about the common roadblocks along the way to a financially comfortable retirement. The last, perhaps, most important, advice we can offer is that you make the journey with an experienced team of professionals who can help you plan and follow your roadmap, providing accurate and insightful directions along the way.

Having read the previous chapters, you can see that retirement planning can get complicated, both financially and legally—especially when you consider the rapid pace of change across the healthcare, financial, tax, regulatory and legal arenas. Here's where a top-notch retirement planning team can be of enormous assistance, because they know this ever-morphing landscape like the back of their hands. They're also experienced in addressing the specific needs of seniors in all kinds of situations. For example:

- *Healthy, vigorous seniors* who want to make sure they remain financially able to maintain their active lifestyle. Poor planning can strip retirees of the lifestyle they once had. I urge you to work with professionals you can trust to make sure you maintain your financial independence. You should be having fun and thriving in your retirement, not scaling back or "moving to a new neighborhood," like we discussed in Chapter 7.

- *Seniors with health problems* or who are facing an uncertain diagnosis. If you're facing health trouble, you need to focus your resources and energy on getting better, not worrying about how to make ends meet financially. As we discussed in Chapters 1 through 3, working with people experienced in guiding others through similar situations can make the difference between total despair and the peace of mind that comes with knowing that any financial problems are being properly addressed.

- *The loved ones of seniors or retirees,* particularly those appointed power of attorney, who want to make sure they understand how to provide asset protection for their spouse, life partner or parent(s). Again, working with a team of financial and legal professionals through this process can make the difference between confusion or uncertainty and the confidence of knowing you're "doing right" by your loved one.

HOW DO YOU FIND THESE TRUSTED GUIDES?

Rather than hunting down separate financial and legal advice, I recommend that you find an experienced team of specialized

---

Rather than hunting down separate financial and legal advice, I recommend that you find an experienced team of specialized professionals.

---

professionals. For example, a financial planner who has strong working relationships with an estate lawyer, professional care-givers, a CPA, and so on—each specializing in one of more aspects of financial planning, estate planning, long-term care, Medicare, Medicaid and the healthcare system in general.

After all, one professional can't wear all of these hats and excel at all of these jobs. However, a team of like-minded people can focus on meeting the overall goals and objectives of the client. Here are a few tips for finding the right guides for your journey:

1. If it sounds too good to be true, it probably is.

It's a common and scary trend today to hear seniors who have made poor decisions based on "buying into great opportunities." For instance, if a financial salesperson tells you about a 9% CD when you know darn well the bank down the road is paying 1.25% on CDs, guess what? That's a red flag—a giant, waving red flag.

When you hear something that sounds good and you want to believe it, ask the person this simple question: "So, what are the strings attached?" If they say "no strings," then you need to turn and run.

There are a lot of great financial products with attractive features. But even the great opportunities out there come with "rules" (aka "strings attached"). You need to know what they are and if they are acceptable to you and in line with your planning goals. Always use and trust your own good judgment and common sense.

2. Watch out for legal advice from non-lawyers.

We know the value of integrating trust documentation and specific financial products. However, be very cautious when the purchase of a financial product also entitles you to free legal documents to support the plan. This is where you can be penny-wise and fortune-foolish.

A key defense from having your money snatched is to

If you enter the keyword "revocable trust" on Google, you'll come up with about 962,000 articles, websites and "resources" to look at.

---

realize legal documents cost money; and a packaged offer with legal documentation included (based on the purchase of a product) should be a giant red flag.

3. Beware of online "resources."

Information online should be viewed with a very skeptical eye. Today it is not uncommon for retirees to jump online to do "research." The critical question is, are you getting information from a credible source? This can be very difficult to decipher online.

Information overload is another problem. If you enter the keyword "revocable trust" on Google, you'll come up with about 962,000 articles, websites and "resources" to look at.

The problem is, before you finished looking at 962,000 online entries, you'd be dead and your family would be burdened by the cost and time delay of probate! (Obviously this would defeat your original planning goal.)

Yes, you need to do research, but on the right thing – finding the right help. Focus your due diligence on finding the right planning team to assist you.

4. Assess how accomplished the potential advice-givers are.

There's nothing worse than getting sold a bad idea. Slick talk can be very persuasive, but it may prove financially disastrous. When seeking professional advice, we recommend that you assess just how accomplished your potential advice-givers really are. A couple of examples:

- *Are they well-known and well-regarded in their community and their industries?* Whether it's from media coverage or plain old word of mouth, people generally build a good name for themselves when they really know their stuff. Media outlets, for example, are looking for real experts because they want their viewers, readers or listeners to get credible and accurate information. Like you, they're looking for someone who doesn't just talk a good game, but who really knows what they're doing – who believes in it strongly enough to go on record with their knowledge and insights.

- *Do they invest in their professional knowledge?* This question is a great way to gauge the prospective advisor's commitment to staying current on new laws, tax code changes and cutting-edge ideas to help preserve and grow your wealth. Same goes for lawyers. If you have a large IRA, you might be swayed knowing an advisor has trained with a recognized expert CPA in the area of IRA planning.

5. Be smart and trust your feelings.
Much is revealed when you meet face to face. See how you feel. We believe that every person who walks through our office

---

Find a team that fully understands

and "owns" your concerns,

challenges and priorities.

---

doors should be treated as if they are members of our own family, and other practices do business in the same way. Sure, credentials are important, but so is your gut feeling. Do you trust these people to help you design and navigate the road plan to your financial future? If the answer is no, keep looking for the right fit.

Find a team that fully understands and "owns" your concerns, challenges and priorities. That's the level of confidence, security and trust you need – and deserve – for complete peace of mind about this immensely important aspect of your life.

I wish you safe and happy travels in your journey to a secure retirement

INDEX

R

revocable living trusts 54-58

S

separately managed accounts (SMAs) 74, 80-82

skilled care 19-20, 38, 43, 46

Social Security 10, 46, 59-64, 68

"spend-down" 23-34, 39, 47-48, 53, 57-58

T

trusts 41-42, 54-58, 59-64

W

wills 43-48, 49-53